NIGHT CREATURES

Animals That Swoop, Crawl, and Creep while You Sleep

Rebecca E. Hirsch

Illustrated by **Sonia Possentini**

A cool night breeze
blows softly
on your face
as night creatures wake
in quiet dens
and dusky nooks.

As day slowly
grows
dark,
and one by one,
stars appear,
night bugs blink on:

flickering,

glimmering

in the dimming light.

Night creatures crouch
in shadows,

creep,

LEAP!

And race out of reach.

Night creatures veer
past night-dark trees:

flapping,

swooping,

catching beetles in flight.

They prowl
for food:

sniff,

reach,

and feast on sweetness.

They squish in muck
in search of fish.

They sound a lonely note:

gaLUNG!

Under the sparkling night sky,
they watch
with yellow eyes,

pluu-u-u-nge—

POUNCE!

And snatch mouse for supper.

Then,
one by one,
stars disappear,
and night slowly

grows

light.

A bird sings:
cheeriup-cheerily-cheeriup,
a song that tells you
morning is here.

Night creatures return
to quiet dens

and dusky nooks,

where they sleep,
until a cool night breeze
blows softly again.

MORE ABOUT NIGHT CREATURES

When you go to bed, many animals are just waking up. Some of these animals are most active at twilight, the period of low light after sunset and before sunrise. We call them crepuscular (krih-PUH-skyuh-luhr). Others are most active in the dark of night. We call them nocturnal (nahk-TUR-nuhl). And still other animals are active in daylight, just like you. The word for them is diurnal (die-UR-nuhl). You'll find all three types in this book.

FIREFLY
crepuscular

Fireflies, also called lightning bugs, are beetles that light up part of their abdomen to attract mates. As the sun goes down, a male flies around and flashes a specific blinking pattern. A female waits in trees, shrubs, or grass. She responds by flashing her own light. The male sees her pattern and flies to her.

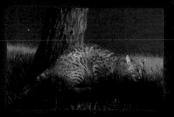

BOBCAT
crepuscular

For a few hours after dusk, bobcats patiently stalk and pounce prey, especially cottontail rabbits. In the darkest part of the night, bobcats rest under rock ledges, in brush, in hollow logs, and under low-hanging tree branches. They hunt again for a few hours at dawn. Bobcats are good at hiding and are rarely seen by people.

COTTONTAIL RABBIT
crepuscular

During the day, cottontail rabbits sleep in shrubs and thickets. When the sun goes down, they come out to nibble grasses, clover, and garden vegetables. As a rabbit eats, it scans for enemies with its sensitive nose, keen ears, and wide-set eyes. If it senses danger, a rabbit may freeze in place to avoid detection or run fast to escape.

BIG BROWN BAT
nocturnal

During the day, big brown bats hang upside down in dark attics and barns, behind shutters, and in hollow trees. At night, they hunt in the dark using echolocation. A bat lets out a stream of high-pitched squeaks. The sound waves bounce off branches, buildings, and flying insects. By listening to the echo, a big brown bat can navigate around objects while scooping flying insects out of the air.

STRIPED SKUNK
nocturnal

In daylight, striped skunks sleep in dens lined with leaves. At night they look for insects, small animals, and fruit to eat. On summer nights, you may see a mother skunk teaching her young how to find food. A skunk's bold stripes, visible at night, warn predators to stay away. But if an enemy comes too close, a skunk will turn away, lift its tail, and release a foul-smelling spray.

RACCOON

nocturnal

During the day, raccoons sleep on tree limbs, inside hollow trees, and in tall grasses. At night they wade along rivers, streams, and ponds in search of fish, crayfish, and frogs to eat. Raccoons will also eat bird eggs, insects, nuts, berries, and even garbage. Raccoons often wet their food before they eat it. Water makes their front paws more sensitive to touch, which helps them identify their food.

NORTHERN GREEN FROG

nocturnal

Green frogs live in ponds, streams, and marshes. They may be brown or tan, as well as green. They hide in plants along the shore eating insects, spiders, and other prey that happens by. At night, male green frogs call to attract a mate. Their mating call sounds like the twang of a plucked banjo string. Females swim slowly by before choosing a mate.

GREAT HORNED OWL

nocturnal

Great horned owls hunt from a high perch and swoop to catch prey in their sharp claws. They have big eyes for spotting prey in low light. They use their keen ears, hidden under their feathers, to detect and pinpoint sounds. Great horned owls are silent in flight, thanks to the soft, fringed edges of their wing feathers. Many people out at night have been startled by an owl silently swooping in front of them.

DEER MOUSE

nocturnal

During the day, deer mice nest in hollow logs, beneath rocks, and in abandoned birds' nests high in trees. At night they search for seeds, fruits, insects, and other food. Deer mice are plentiful, and a female mouse may have thirty young in a year. Deer mice are prey for bobcats and skunks, as well as great horned owls.

AMERICAN ROBIN

diurnal

Robins are one of the first birds to sing in the morning. Before the sun is up, a male robin repeats a loud, whistling call. He sings to court a female and to declare his territory. Once the sun is up, robins search on the ground for insects, worms, and fruit to eat. At night, they sleep in trees and shrubs.

WHITE-TAILED DEER

crepuscular

By day, deer sleep curled on the ground in woods, tall grasses, or thickets. A fawn's white spots help it blend in with the dappled shade of the forest. Before sunrise and after sunset, deer come out of hiding to eat leaves, twigs, fruits, and nuts. You may see female deer, called does, together with fawns. Male deer, or bucks, live in separate groups.

For Robin, Rabbit, and Raccoon,
my nighttime explorers —R.E.H.

To Mia, Nina, and Andrea,
my guides in the day and in the night —S.P.

Millbrook Press™
An imprint of Lerner Publishing Group, Inc.
241 First Avenue North
Minneapolis, MN 55401 USA

For reading levels and more information, look up this title at www.lernerbooks.com.

Designed by Kimberly Morales.
Main body text set in Oldbook ITC Std Bold.
Typeface provided by International Typeface Corporation.
The illustrations in this book were created with pastel, gouache, and colored pencils.

Library of Congress Cataloging-in-Publication Data

Names: Hirsch, Rebecca E., author. | Possentini, Sonia M. L., illustrator.
Title: Night creatures : animals that swoop, crawl, and creep while you sleep / Rebecca E. Hirsch ; illustrated by
    Sonia Possentini.
Description: Minneapolis : Millbrook Press, [2021] | Includes bibliographical references. | Audience: Ages 5–10 |
    Audience: Grades 2–3 | Summary: "As the sun sets, night creatures awaken to hunt, fly, race, leap, and more.
    A mother and child camp out in their rural backyard among the nocturnal animals in this evocative and
    informative picture book" —Provided by publisher.
Identifiers: LCCN 2020057832 (print) | LCCN 2020057833 (ebook) | ISBN 9781541581296 |
    ISBN 9781728430928 (ebook)
Subjects: LCSH: Nocturnal animals—Juvenile literature.
Classification: LCC QL755.5 .H565 2021 (print) | LCC QL755.5 (ebook) | DDC 591.5/18—dc23

LC record available at https://lccn.loc.gov/2020057832
LC ebook record available at https://lccn.loc.gov/2020057833

Manufactured in the United States of America
1-47328-47955-1/22/2021